# The Glass Bead Game

*Volume 3: Wardancing*

Paul Pilkington

# The Glass Bead Game

*Volume 3: Wardancing*

'In open fields that used to fill with dancers,
they lay in heaps.
The country's blood now filled its holes,
like metal in a mould;
Bodies dissolved – like fat left in the sun.'
Sumerian poem, circa 2,000 B.C.

*Cover picture: The Kouretes dance what is likely to be a pyrrhiche
with swords and shields around the infant Zeus,
the tiny seated figure, less than knee height
between the first and second figures on the left*

978-1-873818-06-0
© Abime Publications 2011

# 1 Introduction

This volume explores the four subject matter areas of War, Poetry, Dance and Cookery.

It is striking that man's endeavours and achievements in each of these subject areas have been cited as being unique to humans, and in some cases as a significant defining characteristic of the human condition.[1] In each case, however, the boundary between the animal and human condition is not as clear as might be expected, and as additional observations of animal behaviour continue to accrue, the redefinition of what remains peculiarly human in these areas will no doubt remain the subject of ongoing debate and revision.[2]

In each subject area, humans have developed from instinctive behaviour, through ritualised performance, to purposeful application of emergent principles of order in the service of achieving consciously formulated objectives. Appropriate principles having been established for each subject area within a particular cultural context, we see the persistence and development of these rules, subject to occasional paradigm shifts.[3] Claims are still made for elements of universality within each area, against a common contemporary view of cultural relativity which rejects such

---

[1] Humans as the only species to kill their own kind for reasons other than survival (for example Thomas Hobbes in Leviathan lists the three principle causes of quarrel as competition and gain, diffidence and safety, glory and reputation, and finds the roots of war in the nature of man), the only species to be able to move in time to music (Pinker, S., The faculty of language: what's special about it?, Cognition 95, 2005, p211), the only species with such a complex language faculty (Gentner, T.Q. et al, Recursive syntactic pattern learning by songbirds, Nature, vol 440, 27 April 2008, p1206), and the suggestion that 'the introduction of cooking may well have been the decisive factor in leading man from a primarily animal existence into one that was more fully human.' (Coon, C., The History of Man: From the First Human to Primitive Culture and Beyond, New York, 1954, cited in Reay Tannahilll, Food in History, Eyre Methuen, 1973).

[2] In fact, evolutionary biologists since Darwin have had less interest in differentiating human behaviour, though such a difference necessarily remains a defining foundation of human sciences. Darwin himself is quoted by Marcus, G.F., in Startling Starlings, Nature, vol 440, 27 April 2008, p1118: 'throughout nature almost every part of each living being has probably served, in a slightly modified condition' in some ancestor or another.

[3] For example, the genesis of battle formation or the later proliferation of the use of gunpowder and firearms in war, or the advent of writing or qualitative and quantitative scansion in poetry, or crop cultivation or the use of pottery vessels in cookery, or the development of notations for dance movements (e.g. the Benesh or Laban systems).

universals[4] regardless of which taxonomies and hierarchies of organisation continue to be proposed to organise the subject matter areas.

A recent study of culture in the Classical Athenian City shows an intimate connection existed between the four subject areas under consideration here. And at the dawn of western recorded history, ancient Sparta provides an interesting opportunity to study the four subject matters within a particular culture, as some anthropologists would advocate is the only legitimate approach.[5]

> 'In its commonest form, *mousike* represented for the Greeks a seamless complex of instrumental music, poetic word, and co-ordinated physical movement [... and] was an endlessly variegated, rich set of cultural practices, with strongly marked regional traditions that made them a valuable item of local self-definition as well as a means for exchange and interaction [...] the great war-lord of classical western Greece, Hieron of Syracuse, engaged Pindar, Bakkhylides, and Aiskhylos in an orgy of *mousike* designed (among other things) to beautify the brutality of his activities, which included ethnic cleansing and forced migration on a grand scale. Even so, the poet could mobilize the power of *mousike* to act as a control on the megalomaniac: "no lyres in banquet halls welcome him [viz the bad tyrant] in gentle fellowship with boys' voices" [Pindar, Olympian Ode, 1. 97-98].'[6]

---

[4] Foley, W., Anthropological linguistics, Blackwell, 1997, p169

[5] The anthropological method of F. Boas would, in the terms of the glass bead game table of correspondences, play a single culture in a row across all columns of the table, with each column representing different elements of a culture (as in move 4 of the game in this volume, concerning ancient Sparta), as opposed to playing a single element of culture across all columns, with each column representing different cultures (as in example 2.1.1.2 in volume 1, concerning Irish and Mayan archaeo-astronomy). See, for example, Boas, F., Introduction to the Handbook of American Indian Languages, University of Nebraska Press, 1966 [1911].

[6] Murray, P., Wilson, P. (eds), Music and the Muses: The Culture of Mousike in the Classical Athenian City, OUP, 2004, pp1 - 3

# 2 The four domains of play

## 2.1 War

'Genuinely coalitional aggression is very rare in the animal world. It seems to have evolved only twice, once in the line of primates that has ended in ourselves, and before that among the ants. [...] It is rare because co-operative behaviour is normally restricted to kinship groups [...] and only the social insects have broken that barrier by creating closely related kin groups of enormous size. A tropical anthill may contain 20 million ants, but all except one are siblings, and the colony behaves and evolves like a single organisation. [...] In the ant world, all-out combat between two neighbouring communities for territory, food stores and slaves, often ending in the extinction of one of them, is so common that it seems a forced move. [...] Humans did not practice the ant kind of warfare until they lived in communities that resemble anthills – sedentary, densely populated, rigorously organised, highly territorial. Such human anthills did not appear until the rise of the first agrarian civilisations five thousand years ago, and it will be argued that even after such societies arose, it was many centuries before they began to wage offensive territorial wars against one another.'[7]

It has been suggested that not all human societies have been warlike, though with the development of conditions of scarcity of resources even apparently pacified societies tend to resort to war.[8] Given the weaker kinship in human groups, other conditions have proved sufficient to favour the evolution of warlike behaviours. Study of chimpanzees, which can exhibit planned and orchestrated violence, has identified three characteristics which they have in common with humans, which suffice to lead to such behaviour: organised, male retentive, mildly polygynous social groups with moderate sexual dimorphism[9] (therefore it pays for males to co-operate with one another and compete as a group with other brotherhoods to defend their territory and females); relatively dense populations compared to other

---

[7] Dawson, D., The First Armies, Cassell, 2001

[8] For example the Clovis Paleo-Indian nomads of North America, where a 5,000 year archaeological record shows no evidence of warfare, until gradual settling of the growing population, coupled with soil erosion and water scarcity, eventually led to warlike behaviours and the subsequent abandonment of the tribal lands. (Haas, J., The Origins of War and Ethnic Violence, in Carman, J., and Harding, A., Ancient Warfare, Sutton, 1999)

[9] i.e. males having more than one female partner, and the existence of a systematic difference in form between individuals of different sex in the same species.

primates (such that competition for resources is fiercer); and a level of social intelligence which 'can imagine what other animals are thinking and can attribute intentions to them; they can picture other possible worlds and design alternative scenarios; they can empathise; they can practise deception and cruelty. Only that sort of social cognition makes possible genuine coalitional behaviour, for an effective coalition cannot be forged without the ability to assess the capacities and loyalties of its members.'[10]

Carl von Clausewitz, author of the seminal book *On War*, which codified a type of war current between the French revolution and the 20th century's World Wars, asked of war, 'what is it for?' The answer von Clausewitz offered was limited to his time and place.[11] Chris Hables Gray cites Susan Mansfield's psychological reasons for war:

> "[...] a human institution which satisfies deep-seated psychic needs (the infantile desire for revenge on powerful parents, the anxiety-based insatiability for goods and power, a paranoid sense of powerlessness, etc) and as a ritual attempt to force nature and the divine (the environment) to conform to human will.'[12]

Von Clausewitz would certainly recognise the important role of human will in forcing conformity from the 'friction' of uncertain events of war – and his private correspondence attests that he would recognise it as pleasurable[13] – but he would not acknowledge this as the purpose, merely a necessary ingredient in the successful conduct of war.

As far as ritual is concerned, 'war was a religious act to [Western] classical societies. Armies conducted sacrifices at all stages of a campaign, even on the battlefield with the enemy a few hundred yards away.'[14] In the East, formal styles of warfare were important. Even the most fluid and mobile of armies, the Mongols, were trained in formal manoeuvres in ritual hunts. The development of gunpowder weapons challenged this formality, and as a result the Chinese by mutual

---

[10] Dawson, D., ibid, p34

[11] Von Clausewitz's formulation, 'War is politics by other means', was reversed by Michel Foucault to reflect his view of our own times as politics and power being 'war continued by other means', both cited in Gray, C.H., Postmodern War, Guilford Press, 1997

[12] Mansfield, S., The Gestalt of War: An Inquiry into its Origin and Meaning as a Social Institution, Dial Press, 1982, p19

[13] Von Clausewitz, C., On War (Editor's Introduction), Penguin, 1982 [1832], p22

[14] Herwig, H., et al, Cassell's World History of Warfare, Cassell, 2003, 'War and Society in the Classical West'

agreement deferred the widespread adoption of firearms, and the warring classes in Japan even chose not to use firearms for two centuries after 1637, for social, aesthetic and cultural reasons.[15]

With regard to the importance of order in war, Arthur Ferrill suggests that '"organised warfare" can best be defined with one word. The word is *formation*. [...] When warriors are put into the field in formation, when they work as a team under a commander or leader rather than as a band of leaderless heroes, they have crossed the line (it has been called "the military horizon") from "primitive" to "true" or "organised" warfare.'[16] John Keegan also emphasises order in battle, and points out that the fundamental purpose of training 'is to reduce the conduct of war to a set of rules and a system of procedures – and thereby to make orderly and rational what is essentially chaotic and instinctive.'[17]

One of the earliest known records of organised warfare is the Standard of Ur, dating from about 2,500 B.C., during the Sumerian civilisation in modern day southern Iraq.

> 'The sense of discipline and commitment [...] revealed by the military formations employed, is strongly conveyed. [...] The suggestion of a phalanx, or tight infantry formation, is strongly suggested by their overlapping spears. [...] Overall, it can be suggested that this Sumerian army was a well-disciplined and cohesive force, relying on an early battle car manoeuvre to create gaps in a particular area of the enemy line, which would then be exploited by the weight and discipline of the tightly structured formation of the spearmen. These would advance and thrust their spears in unison to provide maximum impact on the enemy and, at the same time, maximum protection for each spearman.'[18]

While there was not strict standardisation of weaponry, any individual fighting unit operating as a cohesive force must have displayed a degree of consistency in both the design and combination of weapons used, and particular cultures standardised on different designs and combinations. In the ancient Greek city-states, the citizen soldier was called a hoplite, which was named after a particular type of shield used by the troopers. On a broader scale, the weapon technology of an opponent can influence the choice of technology deployed to oppose it, giving rise to the classic

---

[15] Herwig, H., ibid, Eastern Styles of Warfare, p212

[16] Cited by Gray, C.H., Ferrill, Arthur, The Origins of War: From the Stone Age to Alexander the Great, Thames and Hudson, 1985

[17] Cited by Gray, C.H., Keegan, John, The Face of Battle, Penguin, 1976, pp18-19

[18] Herwig, H., ibid, Introduction: The Origins of Warfare

weapon combinations such as spear/sword and shield, and fuelling the arms race ever since.[19] Particular manoeuvres also have a standard response, both at the level of the individual combatants, as well as at other levels of the combat up to overall military strategy.

The integration and ordering of the diverse elements from the entire gamut of possibilities of fighting capability was achieved with varying degrees of success in different cultures. The Assyrian and Persian armies both fielded combined forces drawn from across their vast empires, but while the Assyrians proved 'very clever at organising an integrated army, which dovetailed shock, missile, mobile, and siege troops (infantry, archers and slingers, chariots, cavalry, and siege engineers) into a single effective force,' the Persian army on the other hand 'was really a conglomeration of levies from across the vast empire, each infantry army fighting according to its own tradition, and thus there was an important lack of integration and cohesion among the infantry units.'[20]

Such tight organisation of the military unit as the Sumerian army was not seen again until a millennium later, with the hoplites of the Greeks, Spartans and Macedonians. We don't know the particular rhythm of the hoplite, but we do know the Spartans, the most accomplished and professional soldiery of the region and era, valued a sense of rhythm highly, and cultivated it alongside weapon technique. A warrior's 'sense of rhythm was educated by marching songs and by the energetic dances performed at the annual round of religious festivals.'[21]

Without in any way retreating from the general principle that successful warfare is dependent on order, it must be acknowledged that 'in the heat of battle, plans will go awry, instructions and information will be unclear and misinterpreted, communications will fail, and mistakes and unforeseen events will be commonplace [...] The occurrences of war will not unfold like clockwork. Thus, we cannot hope to impose precise, positive control over events. The best we can hope for is to impose a general framework of order on the disorder, to prescribe the general flow of action rather than to try to control each event. If we are to win, we must be able

---

[19] Though it is not just about developing a weapon which is better than the enemy's, but also adopting a suitable style of warfare: 'Just as sixteenth century knights had to abandon their heavy suits of armour when they faced the new threat of gunpowder, so the strategy to combat IEDs [improvised explosive devices] involves much more than developing protection.' Countering the IED threat, Defence Policy and Business, 28 Jul 2009. Modern day cyberwarfare is another example of adaptive attack and defence.

[20] Herwig, H., ibid, pp24, 35

[21] Plato, Laws 8:6B, cited by Cartledge, P., Hoplites and Heroes, The Journal of Hellenic Studies, v97, 1977

to operate in a disorderly environment. In fact, we must not only be able to fight effectively in the face of disorder, we should seek to generate disorder for our opponent and use it as a weapon against him.'[22]

## 2.2    Dancing

'Informal observations suggest that no other primate can easily be trained to move to an auditory beat, as in marching, dancing, tapping the feet, or clapping the hands. This is surely one of the most elementary characteristics of the human rhythmic response, and one that is displayed spontaneously by young children.'[23] Animals can move rhythmically of course, but evidently not in time to an auditory beat.

The debate continues on whether the bee dance can be classified as communication, given that it is structurally flat and lacks significant complexity, but it is certainly recognisable as a dance. Other animals also dance, including 'birds, and various mammals' courtship interactions', and the predecessors of man are likely to have danced. [24]

> 'As humans evolved, the programmed-action sequences characteristic of other animals – for example a bird's mating display – tended to be replaced by actions in which cultural learning and individual choice played a greater role than instinct. As a specific language has culturally patterned words, sentences and paragraphs, a specific dance has a culturally patterned movement vocabulary, steps and phrases.' [25]

Critical dance scholarship is a relatively new discipline, which begins to ask, in a style characteristic of the Glass Bead Game player:

> 'How do the meanings arising from the performance of various dance styles change as those styles migrate across national, racial, or class boundaries? [...] How are codified movement systems such as dance similar to or different from other forms of representation, such as language or visual representation?'[26]
>
> 'How did the structured movement systems originate? Are they codified into genres? How and by whom can dances be composed? How can

[22] Warfighting, The U.S. Marine Corps Book of Strategy, Currency Doubleday, 1994

[23] Pinker, S., The faculty of language: what's special about it?, Cognition 95, 2005, p211

[24] Garfinkel, Y., Dancing at the Dawn of Agriculture, Texas, 2003

[25] Harris, J.L., 'Cultural Context' in Cohen, S.J. (ed), International Encyclopedia of Dance, Oxford, 2004. In its structure and content, this claim amounts to a Glass Bead Game move.

[26] Desmond, J.C., Meaning in Motion, Duke, 1997

(and cannot) movements and postures be combined? Is there a vocabulary of motifs and a grammar for their use? Are there notions about energy and how it should be visually displayed? On the basis of movement, can dance by separated from ritual? And more basic still, does a culture have such concepts?'[27]

'How does the subject being studied relate to other aspects of that culture? How does this case compare with the situation in other cultures? What does this information reveal to us about human life? What does human dance share, if anything, with the ritual movement of animals? Is there anything universal about how dance is structured, or about how emotions and thoughts are transformed into movement?'[28]

The prevailing contemporary view is that 'all cultures and their dances have unique histories, and that broad categories of dance, representing progressive levels of complexity or stages of civilization, do not exist.'[29] For example, not all societies have had an indigenous notion of recreational dance, as suggested by the widespread adoption of the etymologically obscure French word *danser* to connote the idea as it has been exported to other cultures. 'Because the meaning of movement is culturally patterned, dance is not a universal language. Dance signs may promote self-identity, prescribe social values and roles, and evoke emotion that rallies people to action.'[30]

However, Eastern European researchers, for example, have had a particular interest in analysing dance types in a comparative framework, using a hierarchy of movement units analogous to the word-phrase-sentence structure of language.[31] Elsewhere, a case has been made for a universal generative grammar of dance: 'Following Noam Chomsky and analyses of poetic meter, Singer developed a theory of metrics that proposed that dances are "generated by the encoding of abstract metrical patterns into an organised sequence of movements."' [32]

In her article on Tongan dance[33] Kaeppler defines four structural levels of dance. 'Kinemes' are the smallest elements of movement recognized as significant by the

[27] Lewis, J.L., Ring of Liberation, Deceptive Discourse, in Brazilian Capoeira, University of Chicago, 1992

[28] Youngerman, S., 'Anthropology', in Cohen, S.J., ibid

[29] Harris, J.L., 'Cultural Context', in Cohen, S.J., ibid

[30] Harris, J.L., ibid

[31] Youngermann, S., ibid

[32] Kaeppler, A., 'Linguistics', in Cohen, S.J., ibid

[33] Kaeppler, A., Method and Theory in Analyzing Dance Structure with an Analysis of Tongan Dance, Ethnomusicology, v16. 1972, p173

people who perform a dance tradition, and she compares them to phonemes in language. 'Morphokines' are meaningful movements composed of one or more kinemes. A 'motif' consists of a combination of morphokines that forms an entity. The fourth level is that of the 'genre' itself. As Kaeppler says: 'only a small segment of all possible movements are significant in any single dance tradition.' The idea of certain basic elements of movement has also been central to attempts to notate the dance – notably by Rudolf and Joan Benesh, and separately by Rudolf Laban. 'The movement alphabet complete, steps join up into the phrases of enchainements. These grow into dances.'[34]

Ceremonial dance is a major category of dance, even today ranging from morris dancing to whirling dervishes, with long traditions in many of the world's most ancient cultures.

Western Classical cultures revered dance and made much use of it in ceremony. The Spartans did not compete in the Olympic games, reportedly for fear of tarnishing their reputation for excellence in martial arts. That is, except in dancing, because their military training emphasized moving as a single entity, and was so well ingrained that it made them unbeatable in dancing competitions. One dance in particular, the *pyrrhiche*, 'possibly because of its striking warlike character, has a special place as one of the best documented among ancient Greek dances [... and] was performed by dancers equipped with weapons, that "imitates the modes of avoiding blows and missiles by dropping or giving way, or springing aside, or rising up and falling down; also the opposite postures which are those of action, as, for example, the imitation of archery and the hurling of javelins, and of all sorts of blows" (Plato, Laws, 7.815ab).'[35] In the opinion of Paola Ceccarelli, by the Classical period the pyrrhiche had ceased to be used for real military training, but it still retained an important symbolic value.

In social dancing, closely knit crowds, varying rhythmic patterns in music, switching partners for each dance, and a large vocabulary of movements encourage elements of improvisation in dance. In dance traditions which do not explicitly allow for improvisation, the same variations of music, partners, and individual circumstances of performance necessarily still apply, including the variations of the individual's physical and psychological capability from one performance to the next.

---

[34] Benesh, R. and J., An introduction to Benesh dance notation, Black, 1956

[35] Ceccarelli, P., Dancing the Pyrrhiche in Athens, in Murray, P., Wilson, P. (eds), Music and the Muses: The Culture of Mousike in the Classical Athenian City, OUP, 2004

## 2.3    Poetry

'Contemporary research suggests that the human brain contains few if any unique neuronal types, and few if any genes lack a significant ancestral precedent.  At the same time, humans show much continuity with their non-speaking cousins in dozens of ways that might contribute to language, including mechanisms for representing time and space, for analysing sequences, for auditory analysis, for inhibiting inappropriate action, and for memory.'[36]  'There might be no single property or processing capability that marks the many ways in which the complexity and detail of human language differs from non-human communication systems.'[37]

Some birds such as starlings can learn a basic grammar form, and differentiate between a regular bird 'sentence' and one interrupted by a clause or a phrase.[38] Hauser claims this doesn't disprove the uniqueness of the human faculty for language: the starlings are grasping a basic grammar, but not the necessary semantics to have the language ability that he and Chomsky wrote about.[39]  In a study of the borderline between human utterance and birdsong, Fritz Staal has conducted a structural comparison of certain types of birdsong with Dravidian chant, and has found the 'meaningless' but structured sound sequences of the chant to have more in common with birdsong than with other human languages.[40]

'"Duality of patterning" – the existence of two levels of rule-governed combinatorial structure, one combining meaningless sounds into morphemes, the other combining meaningful morphemes into words and phrases – is a universal design feature of human language.  A combinatorial sound system is a solution to the problem of encoding a large number of concepts (tens of thousands) into a far smaller number of discriminable speech sounds (dozens).  A fixed inventory of sounds, when combined into strings, can multiply out to encode a large number of words, without requiring listeners to make finer and finer analogue discriminations among physically similar sounds.'[41]  It is this combinatorial quality which allows for

---

[36] Marcus, G.F., Startling Starlings, Nature, vol 440, 27 April 2008, p1118

[37] Gentner, T.Q. et al, Recursive syntactic pattern learning by songbirds, Nature, vol 440, 27 April 2008, p1206

[38] Marcus, G.F., ibid

[39] Gentner, T.Q., et al, ibid

[40] Staal, F., Rules Without Meaning: Ritual, Mantras and the Human Sciences (Toronto Studies in Religion, Vol 4), Peter Lang Pub Inc, 1990

[41] Pinker, S., The faculty of language: what's special about it?, Cognition 95 (2005), p211

the rich textures of assonance, alliteration and rhyming which can be found in poetry.

The physical possibilities of the human vocal tract determine the gamut of possible vocal articulations.[42] The FOXP2 DNA sequence, which facilitates the formation of words by the mouth, enabling modern human speech, was possessed by our Neanderthal ancestors at least half a million years ago. 'Most of what distinguishes human language from vocal communication in other species, however, comes not from physical means but cognitive ability.'[43] And a poem, after all, is not made *only* of words[44] but also ideas. Poetry is made of sounds *and content.*

Since Saussure postulated an arbitrary relationship between the sounds of language and its content, others have pointed out important limitations of his assumptions, for example his consideration of language only at a point in time rather than as the evolving complex system it clearly is. The poet J.H. Prynne allows that 'we may if we wish leave arbitrariness in more or less full control of the

---

[42] The International Phonetic Association symbol chart is a systematic transcription of many of the possibilities actually found in languages, including some 'articulations judged impossible' – see e.g. the Encyclopedia of Language and Linguistics, ed. Asher, R.E., Pergamon, 1994, p3050 – though it does not represent the entire gamut of possibilities. Other authors have studied how they are combined in actual languages – e.g. Ladefoged, P., Maddieson, I., The Sounds of the World's Languages, WileyBlackwell, 1995, and Maddieson, I., Patterns of sounds, CUP, 1984. Ladefoged points out: 'We are, of course, aware that there are phonetic phenomena in every language that have yet to be described. Speech varies in response to many different circumstances, and we do not have a complete knowledge of the phonetic structure of any language. In addition, languages are always evolving. Thus there can never be a final description of the sounds of any one language. The next generation of speakers will always speak a little differently from their predecessors, and may even create sounds that have never been used in a human language before. We think it is probable, however, that any new sounds will be similar to those that now have a linguistic function and will be formed by re-arrangements of properties and sounds that have been previously observed in linguistic usage. [...] We have sometimes posited the existence of sounds that have not yet been reported in the linguistic literature. These are sounds which we feel reflect accidental gaps in the currently available data, or are absent only by chance from any currently spoken language. Other possibilities are not mentioned at all since we believe they will never have a role in linguistic structure. There are, of course, many sounds that can be made with the vocal organs that are not known to be used in any language. People can whistle, click their teeth, wag their tongues from side to side, and perform a variety of manoeuvres to produce sounds that have never been reported to have a linguistic function.'

[43] Pollard, K.S., What makes us human? Scientific American, May 2009, p35

[44] *Projective Verse* (1950), collected in Olson, C., Collected Prose, UCP, 1997

central citadel of linguistic theory, but out in the larger semantic fields and forests its writ does not successfully prohibit a wider and more hybrid repertory of contrarious procedures.'[45] In poetry or other language-conscious performance 'the whole prior history of the language-community can be tuned to allow and invite the vibrations of sense and suggestions and historical retrospect. It is not the lexicon which carries these data, so much as the encyclopedia and the historical thesaurus and some ideally synoptic dictionary of quotations: to the functions of language as code and framework have been added those of depot-inventory and memory-theatre.'[46] It is these additional functions which Prynne goes on to call secondary relations, connections or transgressions, and he opines that 'it is the function of a literary context of usage to codify previous innovation into generically part-determined procedures, and to accommodate new innovation by promoting expectancy of such classes of connection.'[47]

Order marks poetry out from common uses of language. Roman Jakobson asked, 'What is the indispensible feature inherent in any piece of poetry? [It is that] the poetic function projects the principle of equivalence from the axis of selection [of words] into the axis of combination [of words].'[48] That is, the poet not only considers selection of words in isolation, but pays far more than usual attention to words in relation to each other. The poem is a phalanx of words, acting rhythmically in co-operation and coalition, and planned and orchestrated to achieve maximum semantic effect.[49] However, poets cannot force language to conform to their will entirely, but can impose a framework of order on the disorder, and should judge when to keep tight control, and when to seek to generate disorder to do its own disruptive work. Prynne, again:

> 'What literate readers can do with literary language is defined not by the permission of rules only, but by their significant secondary transgression, because that too can be intelligibly active as a practice of inscribing new sets of sense-bearing differences upon the schedule of old ones. How far these secondary transgressions can then be allowed to be

---

[45] Prynne, J.H., Stars, Tigers and the Shape of Words, Birkbeck College, 1993

[46] Prynne, ibid. See also Jakobsen below.

[47] Prynne, ibid.

[48] Jakobson, Roman, Linguistics and poetics (1958), in Lodge, D., Modern Criticism and Theory, Longman, 1988

[49] The Battle of the Trees in Robert Graves' White Goddess (Faber, 1948) can be taken as a metaphor for poetry, if trees are in turn a metaphor for (Ogham) letters, as Graves would have us believe. In fact, though a small number of Ogham letters directly designate trees, most of the tree-letter associations are a later medieval construction.

themselves sense-bearing is a function of the interpretative consensus, or of the author/reader contract.[50]

At the same time as enacting a radical letting-go of language through rampant polysemy, and by refusing any semblance of a direct appeal to the reader who is throughout denied any easy illusion or gestalt of meaning, Prynne's poetry[51] attempts a firmer grip by closer attention to the deep etymology of the lexicon (through Middle and Old English, all the way to Proto Indo European) and the ability of the phonemic units of language to bear meaning,[52] and in doing so he consciously grapples with a domain of poetic creation and interpretation usually activated only at a subconscious level.

Jakobson acknowledges that the 'poetic function' is broader than poetry itself. The rules of rhetoric (including repetition, alliteration, assonance, and rhyme) established by the ancient Greeks can be found to have been used extensively by poets from Homer to J.H. Prynne. Some rhetoric is poetry (Caesar's 'Veni, Vidi, Vici'), and some so-called poetry is rhetoric. In his wider definition of the poetic function, Jakobson also cites everyday mnemonic phrases ('Thirty days hath September'), advertising jingles, versified medieval laws, Sanskrit scientific treatises in verse 'which in Indic tradition are strictly distinguished from true poetry', and to Jakobson's list we can add many finely crafted public statements (Churchill's D-Day radio broadcast), some popular catchphrases ('Nice to see you, to see you, nice'), parts of many religious texts (for example the Arabic Qur'an) and sacred and profane ritual (from Callimachus' hymns to contemporary Episcopalian songs), and sub-poetic song lyrics in general.[53]

Jakobson also opines that 'no human culture ignores versemaking, whereas there are many cultural patterns without "applied" verse; and even in such cultures which possess both pure and applied verses, the latter appear to be a secondary,

---

[50] Prynne, ibid. The publication this is extracted from forms part of Prynne's own author/reader contract, and in fact in his poetry the secondary transgressions bear an unusually high proportion of the sense, as the primary system of signification is deliberately effaced.

[51] For example Blue Slides at Rest (2004), in Prynne, J.H., Poems, Bloodaxe, 2005

[52] Prynne, J.H., Mental Ears and Poetic Work, in Chicago Review 55:1, 2010

[53] The following fragment of a lyric is notable in this context because its structure is reminiscent of a glass bead game move: 'Russian roulette isn't the same without a gun. But baby, what's love? If it's not rough, it isn't fun.' Lady Gaga, 2009. What if all glass bead game moves were expressed in poetry which paid as much attention to the language it was presented in, as its content? This hasn't been done, yet.

unquestionably derived phenomenon. The adaptation of poetic means for some heterogeneous purpose does not conceal their primary essence.'[54]

For as long as it has been produced, poetry has also been at the service of rulers wishing to record an official version of events.[55] And if rhythmic dance helped the Spartans to prepare the body, poetry in addition prepared the mind of the warrior with its heroic and moral tales.

> 'The fourth-century Athenian orator Lykourgos tells us that "the Spartans made a law, whenever they went out on campaign, to summon all the soldiers to the king's tent to hear the poems of Tyrtaios, believing that thus they would be most willing to die for their country" (Against Leocrates 107). [...] Like the Spartan custom of *sussitia* (public communal dining), this performance context extended the sphere of commensality in the entire citizen population. In this context, we can imagine the profound effect of verses such as:
>> This is a virtue, this is the best prize among mortals
>> and the most beautiful for a young man to win;
>> And this is a common noble deed for the city and the entire demos,
>> whatever man, planting himself firmly, stands fast in the front ranks
>> unceasingly, and forgets entirely shameful flight,
>> setting at risk his spirit and his enduring heart,
>> and, standing next to his neighbour, encourages him;
>> This one shows himself to be a good man in war. (Tyrtaios, W2 fr. 12, ll. 13-20)'[56]

## 2.4   Cookery

Of all the four subject areas in play, the art of cookery is the closest and most essential to everyday life. 'The senses of smell and taste evolved to evoke strong emotions because they were critical to finding food and mates and avoiding poisons and predators.'[57]

---

[54] Jakobson, ibid.

[55] For example the poetic record of the Battle of Kadesh, 1274 B.C., which praises a heroic victory of Ramses II when other evidence suggests a much more questionable outcome (Warfare of the Ancient Empires, in Herwig, H., ibid)

[56] Taplin, O., Literature in the Greek World, Oxford, 2000

[57] Dr. Jay Gottfried, a neuroscientist at Northwestern University, quoted in a New York Times article 'Cilantro Haters, It's Not Your Fault' by McGee, H., published: April 14, 2010, page D1 of the New York edition

Cookery is often defined as the ordered combination of ingredients, and the application of heat in its preparation. We should include in this definition food preservation through application of ambient heat over a period of time, as in the technique of curing, and the associated addition of preservative and seasoning ingredients.

Animals prepare food in various ways,[58] and can move it from where it is found to storage sites for eating later, or to feed others. Humans, additionally, use techniques of preservation and transformation of ingredients into complex combinations.

'The conquest of fire more than a million years ago and the agricultural revolution about 10,000 years ago made foods high in starch more accessible. But cultural shifts alone were not sufficient to exploit these calorie-rich comestibles. Our predecessors had to adapt genetically to them.'[59] Our DNA is 99% identical to our closest living relative, the common chimpanzee, but differences include the AMY1 sequence which facilitates digestion of starch, which may have enabled early humans to exploit novel foods, and the LCT sequence which modified only 9,000 years ago to permit digestion of milk sugar in adulthood, allowing people to make milk from domesticated animals a dietary staple.

McGee expands further on the cultural significance of milk and cheese: 'The ancient Indo-Europeans were cattle herders who moved out from the Caucasian steppes to settle vast areas of Eurasia around 3000 BCE; and milk and butter are prominent in the creation myths of their descendents, from India to Scandinavia. Peoples of the Mediterranean and Middle East relied on the oil of their olive tree rather than butter, but milk and cheese still figure in the Old Testament as symbols of abundance and creation. [...] Cheese is one of the great achievements of humankind. Not any cheese in particular, but cheese in its astonishing multiplicity, created anew every day in the dairies of the world. Cheese began as a simple way of concentrating and preserving the bounty of the milking season. Then the attentiveness and ingenuity of its makers slowly transformed it into something more

---

[58] See, for example, Byrne, R.W., Object manipulation and skill organization in the complex food preparation of mountain gorillas, in The mentalities of gorillas and orangutans: comparative perspectives, Parker, S.T., Parker, Mitchell, R.W., Miles, H.L., Cambridge University Press, 1999: 'Gorillas eat over thirty different foods [... and] different techniques are involved with each. [...] In texts on human evolution, it is axiomatic to stress the importance of manual dexterity and control, in particularly the retention of the primitive pentadactyl hand in primates and the enhanced flexibility of control in great apes. Primates in the wild show skills of manual precision almost entirely in food preparation and grooming.'

[59] Pollard, K.S., What makes us human? Scientific American, May 2009

than mere physical nourishment: into an intense, concentrated expression of pastures and animals, of microbes and time.'[60]

'In the past the relationship between people and their livestock was much more intimate. The meat of Greek animals is god-given [...] for the Greeks, matters relating to butchery, religion and cooking were all mixed up in what they called *thusia* and what we call *sacrifice*. [...] In the language of Homer, to express the idea of the slaughter of livestock, there are no verbs other than those relating to offering up sacrifices to the gods.'[61] Levi-Strauss also postulates that a group of South American myths he has analysed 'view culinary operations as mediatory activities between heaven and earth, life and death, nature and society.'[62]

With the advent and development of agriculture in the Near East, Central America and China around 10,000 years ago, the hunter-gatherer's diet changed from consuming wild versions of crops and whatever animals could be caught, to a more standardised range of foods which could be successfully cultivated in a given situation. 'A clear shift from marine to terrestrial diets is seen at the start of the Neolithic in Britain (c. 4000 – 2500 BC), for instance, and the arrival of maize is equally clear from carbon isotope ratios in American studies.'[63] Trade routes and availability of foodstuffs also influenced the gamut of foods typically adopted at a particular time and place.

In time, the axis of selection from the available options developed further towards combinations of flavour and foods, in such a way as to allow integration and

---

[60] McGee, H., Food and Cooking, An Encyclopedia of Kitchen Science, History and Culture, Hodder and Stoughton, 2004, p7-8, 51

[61] Detienne, M., Vernant, J.-P., La Cuisine du sacrifice en pays grec, Gallimard, translated and cited in Larousse gastronomique, Hamlyn, 2001, p7

[62] Levi-Strauss, C., The raw and the cooked: introduction to a science of mythology, Jonathan Cape, 1970

[63] Friedman, P. (ed.), Food: the history of taste, Thames and Hudson, 2007. The extract continues: '[An] extreme case relates to early farmers in the South West of the USA. During the 'Pueblo II' phase, dating to around the eleventh century AD, the conditions for maize cultivation were good and the inhabitants of the area ate little else. They had beans as well, but did not do much with them. All the evidence points to an absolutely monotonous diet of corn and more corn. Archaeologists have also noted that they had little variety in the way they cooked it. There are no structures that indicate the production of bread. They just ate ground, boiled, corn. The result was very bad health indeed. They were getting plenty of calories but were deficient in many other nutrients and had lots of dental problems.'

cohesion among the ingredient units within a dish, and further throughout the entire menu.[64]

Many other conventions, rituals and constraints impose another level of order on food selection, though such constraints are easily overcome by creative innovations and improvisations when required by the moment: 'In February 1548 Swiss ambassadors visiting Fontainebleau for the baptism of Claude, seventh child of Henry II and Catherine de Medici, were invited to an "historical" banquet. As this was during Lent, fish was served instead of meat and included lamprey, turtle, trout, char, anchovy, herring, snails, frog paté, carp and eels.'[65]

Recipes are also adjusted to suit particular tastes – 'As Roger Vergé, one of the great French chefs of the world, says: "A recipe is not meant to be followed exactly – it is a canvas on which you can embroider"'[66] – and are adapted to suit the culinary techniques, technology and ingredients of the time. Heston Blumenthal's Meat Fruit is based on a Tudor recipe: a bowl of fruit apparently contains a mandarin, which in fact is made from chicken livers and foie gras covered in a glaze. It is the very precision of the details of the illusion which increases the proportion of indeterminacy and pushes the element of surprise which undermines the reader's ability to successfully form an accurate gestalt of the dish towards a new limit, with the ultimate incompleteness of the illusion (if only on tasting the dish) giving it its productive value. [67]

'Since the earliest times the idea of the communal meal has been associated with a magical rite. Every man had to gain the favour of the mysterious forces of nature to be lucky in the chase; by eating the animal he had killed with his companions, he regenerated his mental and physical strength.'[68] The Spartans recognised the importance of communal dining and cookery in warfare, and established a professional class of cooks. However, Plato (and elsewhere Aristotle[69]) is dismissive of the art by including cookery as a category of 'flattery' (alongside beautification, sophistic and rhetoric as 'having no thought for what is best'), though

[64] Dornenburg, A., and Page, K., Culinary Artistry, John Wiley & Sons, 1996, pp50, 223ff.

[65] Larousse gastronomique, Hamlyn, 2001, p75

[66] Vergé, R., (trans. Conran, C.,), Cuisine of the Sun, Macmillan, 1979, quoted by Rhodes, G., New British Classics, BBC, 1999

[67] '[In modern texts] it is the very precision of the written details which increases the proportion of indeterminacy... The formation of illusions, therefore, can never be total, but it is this very incompleteness that in fact gives it its productive value.' Iser, W., The Reading Process: a phenomenological approach, in New Literary History 3, 1972

[68] Larousse gastronomique, ibid.

[69] Aristotle, Politics, Book I, 7

it nevertheless features as a counterpart of medicine in catering to the body's requirements (Plato, Gorgias, 463 - 465).[70]

Further aspects of the idea of order in cookery are explored in the later section on rhythm in the development of the game.

---

[70] Plato's expression of this relationship in what he calls 'the language of the geometers' (i.e. a proportion) is notable for being in the form of an elegant Glass Bead Game move with eight terms, with a symmetrical structure of four comparisons:

'Sophistic is to legislation in administering to the soul and

Rhetoric is to justice in administering to the soul as

Beautification is to gymnastics in administering to the body and

Cookery is to medicine in administering to the body.'

In each individual comparison, the first term is a species of flattery, which has no thought for what is best, while on the other hand the second term does administer to what is best.

# 3 Development of the game

## 3.1 General observations arising from designing this game

There is no existing literature which draws all these four subject matter areas together, nor any line of writers which has pursued cross-disciplinary studies across these areas, and there are no pre-existing 'tables of correspondences'.[71]

Finding a suitable radial axis is a significant and sometimes difficult task in game design. To a certain extent, after this is done, with systematic research the game comes together relatively easily. In designing this game, after a challenging start, I had multi-dimensional comparisons in abundance, but ultimately they didn't fit into a unifying radial organising principle. I have set out some of these "remaindered moves" in section 5.

## 3.2 The radial axis

Two preoccupations – rhythm and structure – provided the seed for the radial axis, and though neither of these feature in the current game in the form initially conceived, traces of both are discernable in the game which is set out in section 4.

### 3.2.1 Rhythm

'The whole of both physical and mental life is a dynamic phenomenon, of which the Glass Bead Game basically comprehends only the aesthetic side, and does so predominantly as an image of rhythmic processes.'[72]

Regardless of whether humankind may need rhythm and order, we can't avoid it. The primary stable aural sensation of a baby gestating in the womb is its mother's rhythmic heartbeat. One of the first sensory impressions of a baby being delivered into the world must include the absence of this audible heartbeat, and perhaps one of the main joys in life is its rediscovery in audible order, rhythm and dance. The free-swinging body or limb moves in the harmonic motion of Hooke's Law. The able-bodied biped's gait and step is symmetrical and rhythmic, and the quadruped's, though more complex and varied, is equally rhythmic and ordered.

---

[71] See Volume1: A basic form of play, genealogy, and examples. There are, however, more Old Norse and Old English kennings on the subject of battle than perhaps any other area, which is not surprising given the focus on heroic saga in the poetic traditions of these languages.

[72] Hesse, H., The Glass Bead Game, Bantam, 1972 (originally published in German in 1943)

I consciously set out to look for analogous rhythmic structures in the four subject matter domains. Cookery was the subject matter area most resistant to the concept of rhythm – not because rhythm is not applicable to the area, but rather because, on initial consideration, the rhythms of food preparation are on a different timescale from the rhythms by which dance, poetry and battle manoeuvre and movement are organised. The rhythms of cookery are the rhythms of the seasons, agriculture, and preservation of food materials. The preparation of an individual meal has order and structure, but little rhythm except that it all must come together at the right time.

However, it was a deeper consideration of the idea of rhythm in the domain of cookery in particular which led to other temporally-based commonalities which could act as an organising principle across all the four subject domains. Firstly, the passage from animal to modern human behaviour. Secondly the idea of each of these domains featuring events at a point in time which are a culmination of subordinate events of widely varying duration, for example, the ingredients of a given meal might include inorganic material such as salt of ancient vintage, wines and spirits aged for several decades or even centuries, organic produce harvested some weeks or months previously, and fresh produce of a day or less, or even still alive when consumed. Further exploration of rhythm as an organising principle is left to a future game and another occasion, which might take the form of a kind of Fourier analysis of a particular significant contemporary meal, battle, poem, and dance performance, and analyse their constituent elements to identify and examine the provenance of those of some considerable vintage, and those of more recent genesis.

### 3.2.2 Structure

The idea of structure emerging from disorder provides another rich narrative to explore these subject domains. Equally rich is the discourse surrounding the subjectivity of any idea of structure, which is dependent on our viewpoint, as well as the context and environment of the observed phenomenon, such that the idea of order can be understood more as a correlation between observer and subject, rather than anything more objective.

In interesting counterpoint to this idea of emerging order is the concept of entropy, and the second law of thermodynamics which states that any given system will generally become more chaotic, and can only become more ordered when it is acted on by energy more ordered than the system itself. Many have assayed explanations of how life itself is possible[73] in the general context of this 'most pessimistic and amoral formulation in all human thought.'[74] Others seem content to gratefully accept life, culture and structure as an entertaining but transitory 'edge effect' of the inevitable heat death of the universe.

### 3.2.3   The centre of the mandala

It is possible to represent any glass bead game (shown in section 4 as a table) as a mandala.[75] The moves in this game represent increasingly ordered and specific components as they progress towards the outer edge of the mandala (the lower part of the table of correspondences). As such, one nexus of ideas at the centre of the game is the ordering principle working against a backdrop of increasing general disorder known as entropy.

Another significant theme which extends into the centre beyond the first and most central move in the particular game played here is the questionable boundary between man and beast. As John Wilmott, Earl of Rochester opined:

> 'But a meek, humble man of modest sense,
> Who, preaching peace, does practice continence,
> Whose pious life's a proof he does believe
> Mysterious truths which no man can conceive;
> If upon the earth there dwell such God-like men,
> I'll here recant my paradox to them,
> Adore those shrines of virtue, homage pay,
> And with the rabble world their laws obey.
>    If such there are, yet grant me this at least,
> Man differs more from man than man from beast.'[76]

[73] Schrödinger, E.,What is Life? The Physical Aspect of the Living Cell. Cambridge, (2nd edition), 1967; Pauling L (1987) Schrödinger's contribution to chemistry and biology, in Kilmister C.W. (ed), Schrödinger. Centenary Celebration of a Polymath Cambridge, 1987, p225-233; Perutz M.F., Erwin Schrödinger's What is Life? and molecular biology, in Kilmister C.W., ibid, 234-251

[74] Hill, G. and Thornley, K., Principia Discordia, Loompanics, 1979

[75] See volumes 1 and 2 of this series.

[76] Wilmot, J., Earl of Rochester, Selected Works, Penguin Classics, 2004

# 4 The Wardancing game

## 4.1 Move 1 – The gamut of possibilities

The known physical properties of explosives, metals, men and animals are to the martial technology of a particular time and period

As

The physical capability of the vocal tract and mouth are to the phonemic set used in a particular language

As

The physical capability of the body and its joints are to the kinemes of a specific dance culture

And as

The known edible substances and produce (and techniques and norms concerning food preservation) are to the elements used in food preparation in a particular time and place

In each case, the first term exceeds and includes the second, through a process of selection.

Part of any process of ordering physical phenomena is bounding the infinite into the finite by identifying discrete taxa within the continuum, and allowing for individual variation to resolve towards these taxa[77]

## 4.2 Move 2 – Unordered inputs and ordered outputs

Fighters are to formation

As

Words are to a poem

As

Movements are to dance

And as

Ingredients are to cookery

In each case, from the first term emerges an ordering in the form of the second term.

The timing and rhythm of the combination of the elements is crucial in all cases.

---

[77] For more on taxa, see volume 2.

## 4.3 Move 3 – Conventions, rituals and constraints

The grammar or lexicon of set piece manoeuvres and military drill exercises is to the exigencies of a particular battle in the context of friction, uncertainty, fluidity, disorder and the human dimension
As
The norms of composition and common definitions of words are to the 'secondary transgressions' in a particular poem which work differently on every reader
And as
The recipe is to the preparation of a particular meal from the (always different and variable) ingredients at hand in the context of the location, season and quality

In each case, the first term is instantiated by a particular variant in the form of the second term.

An alternative comparison in the dimension of poetry might be: 'generative grammar is to the original speech act.'

## 4.4 Move 4 – Order in the service of war in a particular martial culture

The phalanx is to the technical superiority of Sparta in warfare
As
An exhortation by Tyrtaios is to the motivational superiority of Sparta in warfare
As
The pyrrhiche is to the superior rhythmic coordination of Spartans in formation
And as
A shared meal is to the heightened communal spirit and altruism in Spartans, including warriors

In each case, the first term is associated with and has a causal relationship to the second term.

## 4.5 Summary of the game as a 'table of correspondences'

| | War | Poetry | Dance | Cookery | Nature of the comparison |
|---|---|---|---|---|---|
| 1. The gamut of possibilities: The particular elements in a human culture | Known physical properties of explosives, metals, men and animals : Martial technology of a particular time and period | Physical capability of the vocal tract and mouth : Phonemic set used in a particular language | Physical capability of the body and its joints : Kinemes of a specific dance culture | Known edible substances and produce (and techniques and norms concerning food preservation) : Elements used in food preparation in a particular time and place | exceeds and includes, by selection ... |
| 2. Unordered inputs: Ordered outputs | Fighters : Formation | Words : Poem | Movements : Dance | Ingredients : Cookery | from which emerges an ordering in the form of ... |
| 3. Conventions, rituals and constraints comprising order : Innovations and improvisations required by the moment | Grammar/lexicon of set piece manoeuvres and military drill exercises : Exigencies of a particular battle in the context of friction, uncertainty, fluidity, disorder and the human dimension | Norms of composition and common definitions of words : 'Secondary transgressions' in a particular poem which work differently on every reader | | Recipe : Preparation of a particular meal from the (always different and variable) ingredients at hand in the context of the location, season and quality | Is instantiated by a variant in the form of ... |
| 4. Particular (early) form of order (in service of war): A particular (early) martial culture | Phalanx : the technical superiority of Sparta in warfare | An exhortation by Tyrtaios : the motivational superiority of Sparta in warfare | Pyrrhiche : the superior rhythmical coordination of Spartans in formation | A (shared) meal : heightened communal spirit (and altruism) in Spartans, including warriors | is associated with (has a causal relationship to) ... |

## 4.6 Game commentary

For the first time in these volumes, in the summary table we explicitly see the nature of the comparison in each row, assisting the reader to understand more readily the relation between the comparisons in each subject area.

The first two moves are also 'glossed' with meditations reminiscent of those hinted at in Hesse's own Glass Bead Games.

The brevity of the game allows more coherence in the radial axis compared to games in earlier volumes, and the cultural specificity of the last move, while not particularly well 'prepared' by the cultural generality of the preceding moves, nevertheless stands in pleasing contrast, and clear relation to those moves.

# 5  Further developments

## 5.1  Remaindered moves

There follows a record of various moves which did not fit within the radial axis of this particular game, but which may have some interest in their own right.

### 5.1.1  Binary oppositions

Attack is to defence
As
Consonant is to vowel
As
Movement is to rest
And as
Food is to drink

These are the accepted binary oppositions within each field, which should be considered against the following contexts, which in themselves represent a comparison of sorts across the four disciplines:

- US Marine Handbook: 'While opposing forms, the offence and defence are not mutually exclusive. In fact, they cannot exist separately.'[78]
- Louis Zukofsky on vowels and consonants: 'The vowels/ abide/ in consonants/ like// souls/ in/ bodies.'[79]
- First position in ballet, or ginga in Capoeira[80] both simultaneously containing rest and movement.

---

[78] Warfighting, ibid, p32

[79] Zukofsky, L., 4 Other Countries, from Barely and Widely [1956 – 1958], in Complete Short Poetry, John Hopkins, 1991

[80] 'In the physical domain, the analogue of the buzz note [on the berimbau] is the ginga, out of which all attacks and escapes are born. The ginga is neither attack nor escape, but it contains both. It is said that the advanced player never uses the ginga, but from another perspective everything he does is ginga. Likewise, the ginga, for most players, provides continuity between interchanges, a recovery position from which one is not obliged to either attack or defend (at least for a moment). Both the buzz and the ginga insure the flow of the game – one the musical flow, the other physical flow – providing the smoothness characteristic of capoeira that distinguishes it from many other martial arts.' Lewis, J.L., Ring of Liberation,: Deceptive Discourse in Brazilian Capoeira, University of Chigago Press, 1992, p145

- McGee on milk: 'Milk has long been synonymous with wholesome, fundamental nutrition, and for good reason: unlike most of our foods, it is actually designed to be a food.'[81]

## 5.1.2 The extraordinary leading to the heinous

The gift of the Trojan horse is to the sacking of Troy
As
Timotheus' song is to the firing of the Persian Capital after Alexander's Feast[82]
And as
Salome's dance is to the beheading of John the Baptist

## 5.1.3 Concentration

Combat with a weapon is to unarmed combat[83]
As
Poetry is to prose[84]
And as
Cheese is to milk (or a reduction of a sauce is to its original state, or salt is to flavour) [85]

## 5.2 Unanswered questions

The following aspects must await another occasion for further exploration:

- The analogues in war, cookery and dance of the *sounds* and *content* in poetry, and Robert Creeley's assertion that poetic 'form is never more than an extension of content.'[86]
- The projection of the poetic principle of equivalence from the axis of selection into the axis of combination, onto the fields of war, cookery and dance.

---

[81] McGee, H., ibid, p12.

[82] Dryden, J., Poems and Fables, 1962, Oxford, p504-8: 'The Princes applaud, with a furious Joy;/ And the King seyz'd a Flambeau, with Zeal to destroy;/ Thais led the Way,/ To light him to his Prey,/ And, like another Hellen, fir'd another Troy.'

[83] The weapon concentrates force.

[84] Pound, E., ABC of Reading, New Directions, 1960 [1934], p.36: 'Dichten = condensare. I begin with poetry because it is the most concentrated form of verbal expression. Basil Bunting, fumbling around with a German-Italian dictionary, found that this idea of poetry as concentration is as old almost as the German language.'

[85] McGee, H., ibid

[86] Cited in Olsen, C., Projective Verse (1950), in Collected Prose, UCP, 1997

- The equivalents of common ratio in cookery (e.g. bread is five parts flour to three parts water[87]) to aspects of dance, war and poetry.
- The analogues of the military concepts of fog, friction and chaos[88] in poetry, cookery and dance.
- A 'Fourier analysis' of a contemporary battle, meal, poem and dance, identifying the vintage and provenance of each of its components.

---

[87] Ruhlman, M., Ratio: The Simple Codes Behind the Craft of Everyday Cooking, Scribner, 2009. McGee, H., ibid, has the standard ratio for bread as 65 parts water to 100 of flour.
[88] Warfighting, ibid.